Walking the Fence
Selected Tanka of Randy Brooks

Walking the Fence

Selected Tanka
of
Randy Brooks

Brooks Brooks
Taylorville, Illinois

Walking the Fence: Selected Tanka of Randy Brooks
Copyright © 2019 by Brooks Books
Printed in the United States of America

First Edition

ISBN: 978-1-929820-18-4

Brooks Books
6 Madera Court
Taylorville, Illinois 62568

www.brooksbookshaiku.com
brooksbooks@gmail.com

with deep thanks to

Sandy Goldstein,
who invited me into
this tanka world

Tanka: the Art of Walking the Fence

When I was about five years old, my father challenged me and my brother to a foot race. He said he could beat us using only one foot half of the time. In the race Dad ran the same as always, easily beating us, alternating one foot then the other all the way to the finish line. We complained that it wasn't fair, but he ran in slow motion to show us that only one foot was on the ground at a time throughout the race. Whenever we whined about justice, Dad would say that the world is not a just place, it's just a place. This was an early lesson in metaphysics, language and ethics.

Over the years I often wondered about the foot that was running in the air half the time. I surmised that if one foot was on the ground, the other foot was running in the air. What if both feet could run or walk without touching the ground before the next step? Maybe we are always walking the fence between this world and a world that floats beyond. The first step pushes off from the ground, but what if the second step and additional steps continued into the air without touching the ground?

Walking this fence, without being grounded, requires a great deal of self-confidence and an initial leap of faith that goes beyond our conventional sense of reality. Walking this fence has come to represent my journey into the world of tanka. I walk this fence out of curiosity about things just out of reach, just beyond the visible horizon. Walking the fence requires two steps. After the first step I hold my breath and build up courage for a leap of faith, a second step into that which is beyond the place where I am, into this tanka world.

Walking the fence I know the dirt is beneath me, but I don't have to stay grounded. I can let my tanka lead me to the outer reaches of caring and loving others, or I can let my tanka lead me into the interior spaces within myself. I can write tanka that float over this daily existence into the spirit world of being alive and loving others. Or I can write tanka that lead me to turn inward, pausing for a moment of contemplation, then moving deeper within the soul for a serious talk with myself. Either direction, my tanka are psychological movements. In the best tanka, I journey out into this tanka world and return to earth with a gentle land fall. I want my tanka to move me and my readers so that we can enjoy both the foot running in the air and the one on the ground.

I am not interested in writing tanka that plod along counting steps or syllables. I don't seek flashy words to show off my vocabulary or tricky linguistic gymnastics to show off a mastery of twisted sentences. I am not interested in turning my tanka into word puzzles. I am also not interested in writing waka, following the refinements of stylized beauty and related tropes of the aristocratic traditions. I am not interested in writing tanka based on an algebra of short-long-short-long-long phrases. I am compelled to write tanka out of the Modernist traditions of Takuboku Ishikawa and Akiko Yosano. I want my tanka to be raw and spontaneous expressions of spiritual or psychological journeys written with a voice of authentic, caring conversation between contemporary friends. This is my tanka, the art of walking the fence.

THIS SELECTED TANKA COLLECTION

With the help of my trusted readers, family and friends—Shirley Brooks, Jessica and Jake Sebok, Mary Peters, Carmella Braniger and Aubrie Cox—I have gathered the best tanka I have written over the last four decades. I am also very grateful to the editors who have selected my tanka for publication in their journals and anthologies. Please see the publication credits in the back of this book for complete details of previous publications.

The tanka in *Walking the Fence* are not arranged chronologically, but rather clustered into seven arenas of human experience. (1) I open with "Coyote Pup," a collection of tanka from my childhood memories of growing up in Western Kansas. (2) It has been a deeply rewarding pleasure to be a father and grandfather. I have always enjoyed writing about the joys, surprises and challenges of parenting, so these tanka are collected in the second section titled, "Charms for Parents." (3) Dedicated to my lifelong companion and inspiring wife, Shirley, the third section is called, "Small of Her Back." This section features tanka that explore love and romance. (4) The fourth section, "Dusty Old Bones," features tanka about aging and growing older. It happens. (5) As a college professor, I have enjoyed many years as a teacher, scholar and academic leader. "Campus Rituals" is a small selection of tanka on writing and teaching. (6) I've included a few of the tanka from my online collection, *Black Ant's Journey to Japan*, first published by Jane Reinhold at AHA Books. (7) The concluding section, "Walking the Fence," gathers tanka from my spiritual journey—a chronicle of dreams, prayers and meditations.

MY TANKA JOURNEY

I have been writing tanka since 1977, when I was first introduced to Modernist Japanese tanka writers by Dr. Sanford Goldstein. I was fortunate to be part of a small tanka-writing group led by Sandy at Purdue University. At that time, there were few avenues for publishing English language tanka, so Shirley and I were pleased to publish several tanka in issues of *High/Coo: A Quarterly of Short Poetry*. In 1978 we also published one of the earliest chapbooks of English tanka, *Rain in Her Voice*, by one of the Purdue tanka writers, Gregg Fitzgerald.

In the spring of 2000, Millikin University hosted the Global Haiku Festival. Michael Dylan Welch suggested that this would be an excellent occasion to start a new organization dedicated to English language tanka. I agreed, and it was my pleasure to work with Michael on the founding of the Tanka Society of America as one of our featured events at the festival. About 20 poets participated in that seminal meeting. I have been so pleased to see the growth of interest and expertise in writing and publishing tanka in English over the last four decades.

Although I have introduced many students to tanka in my classes over the years, more recently I have co-taught English language tanka classes at Millikin University with Dr. Carmella Braniger. As a result of these classes, we have had the opportunity to write collaborative tanka sequences with our students and alumni. Although these sequences are not included in this collection, I have included some of my tanka written in this call-and-response method of collaboration. I want to thank Carmella Braniger, Aubrie Cox, Jackson Lewis, Joseph Bein, and Natalie Perfetti for being my inspiring tanka writing partners. The publication credits for these five sequences can lead you to the complete tanka trios and quartets.

I hope my tanka open up memories, feelings, understandings and especially a few smiles as you join me on my journey, walking the fence.

~ *Randy Brooks, April 6, 2019*

Table of Contents

Coyote Pup

thunder
a girl races
ahead of the kite
both feet off
the ground

brittle pages
of the pirate book . . .
my brother
pokes me out
onto the tree house plank

pink lagoon
we hold hands
across the dam
a trickle of water
over our toes

grandpa's
domino
adds up
again
not a grin

all kinds
the freckled boy
smiles
scratching behind
the old mutt's ear

cousin's tracks
left in the snow
the remains
of a game
of fox and geese

snow-covered
sugar cane shocks
tossed into the trunk.
again, my apologies,
mr. and mrs. mouse

me
and my dad
walk the ranch fences
mending everything
by spring

grandpa wades into
the Dodge City pool
in his cowboy hat
we give a whoop and holler
splashing over to his side

crawling through
the overgrown brush
we play war
it's so easy knowing
who the bad guys are

late night swim
giggles
and side-way glances
down the path
to the lake

the voice
from another country
oh Papa
tell me a story
of long ago

prayer meeting
one eye open
to see
the new girl
peeking back at me

cousins calling
my name
over and over
i wait to hear
alli alli all in free

lunch break
a janitor
plays dominoes
with the kid
flunking math

floodwater swirls
across our driveway
I assure my father
I won't let go
of the rope again

I rescue
a carpenter ant
from the swimming pool
the strength to hold on
to a blade of grass

invisible cousins
kissing
in the mulberry tree
plenty of berries
for the sparrows

needle nose tweezers
for a tick
in an intimate place
grandma banishes
the cousins

turkey wishbone
bends and bends
but doesn't break
my wish, your wish
will have to wait

the smooth stone
grandfather handed
down to me
no worry left
in it

a coyote gives us
a hitch across Missouri
his jail release things
in a manila envelope
on the pickup dash

mud line
to the second step
of our porch
somebody's tracks
already home

favorite jokes
and Kansas pranks
my grandpa
just a story
I like to tell

a-ten hut!
the pinup girl salutes
boys headed to war
in the shop over
grandpa's workbench

grandpa gave me
an old key
for keeps
I've been looking
for the lock ever since

Charms for Parents

bottom
of the slide
his feet
hit running
again

about the size
of the cat
when you were
newborn . . .
my son meows

he squirms
and turns
on second base
to hold
it in

first grader's name
scratched
into his bedpost
at least
he spelled it right

right fielder
runs home
opening his mitt
to show us
a tooth

fireworks over
two angels
with crooked necks
asleep
in the back seat

scar on her brow
so easy to recall that day
she fell on the rocks
and I needed to be
the strong one

head back to
catch a
snowflake on
his tongue ~
school bus stops

family around
the breakfast table
little brother's name
etched into
the last banana

left on
the porch steps
a grocery sack
of green apples
and her note

oh shit!
I need to wash
my mouth out
changing
the diaper

Narita Airport
up
against
mother breasts,
the sleeping child

second time
through the spook house
the confidence
of little brother's
guided tour

letter to Santa
she asks us
to check for typos
before putting it
in the mailbox

mother
and daughter's
secret grinning
across supper . . .
oh, her first period

another knot tied
into a clover
necklace
she repeats
the spell of his name

first moon
she takes
her mother's hand
to walk
with grace

the thump
of fireworks
on her face
she signs
for more

a hoot
a hoot
far enough
on the forest path
we turn back

oink oink here
moo moo there
now a couple
of hissing snakes
from the twin's stroller

so many brooks
into the river
into the lake
my father, me, my son,
my granddaughters

brothers suddenly
harmonizing
from years ago
the old mushroom
hunting song

is it flu
or morning sickness?
all I know
is the tenderness
in your eyes

hat, then mittens,
your long red scarf
ah, here you are
cradling a cup
of chicken soup

small fingers open
to the possibility
of your embrace
I want to feel
so light again

a beady eye sewn
on the sock monkey
she hands it
to the little one
who brings it back to life

three charms
against the dark arts:
sweet thoughts
ridiculous
just a movie

bacon and eggs
over easy
when I was your age
we served trolls
wine and cheese

granddaughters squeal
seeking grandpa
through the house
soon they'll master
hiding too

neighborhood girls
call out their positions
the new coach
dusts snowflakes
off home plate

hippie clothes
in the dress-up
closet
my daughter
lets the sunshine in

end of summer
my small town family
grows smaller
in the rear view
mirror

so late for
headlights in the driveway
I decide to
hold on to the words
piling up inside

state fair queen
in the swine barn
the young judge
can't take his eyes
off of you

farmer's daughter
home with her mother
sparrows chirping
back and forth
in the garden

angel hair pasta
our birthday girl
lets the cute waiter
crank and crank
shavings of Parmesan

foul ball
caught by dad
daughter
tosses it back
into play

little girls
hush me!
the daffodils
are telling them
a secret

when I agreed
she could
pierce her ears
thirteen seemed
so far away

pebbles on
the window screen
a boy I don't know
whispers
my daughter's name

prom dress
on a hanger
the strapless top
holds the shape
of my daughter

farm boys
each with a foxtail
after the church potluck
rooster tail of dust
behind the hot rod

Mother's Day
left under an avocado
on the kitchen table
her daughter's declaration
of independence

back home
from the blood test
my granddaughters
show me the different neighs
of a zebra and horse

back and forth
in line
for the roller coaster
more or less
of her tattoo

waiting for the sun
to return
I'm on a short leash
under a pear tree
in full bloom

not a lifesaving ring
she brings a hoe
to cut down
the weeds
in little sister's garden

beer set out
on the back porch
a Trojan horse
for her gossipy
neighbor boys

after church
at the restaurant
he asks for our blessing
of the word
boyfriend

bookshop cat
asleep on the counter
my daughter
asks
for a job

bacon and eggs
for my daughter
any minute now
she'll be off
to college

Small of Her Back

friday night football . . .
that freckle-faced
clarinet winked
at me
oh yes she did

into
the bean field
into the moonlight she
takes me by
the hand

on our backs
looking up through
the summer night
a firefly
connects the dots

behind her
up
the hayloft
I watch
my step

endless rows
of weeds
between the beans
ah, the whole long day
with my lover

rain
on the window
talking
to myself
for you

tangled sheets . . .
my wife's legs grow longer
with each
night's
dream

silver moon
here too soon . . .
warmth leaving
her side
of the bed

first the eyes
then the gestures
of her hands
how long can I pretend
not to understand?

daffodils up . . .
my wife
puts my hand on
the small
of her back

Route 66
one mile, two
how many miles
till I'm back
with you?

the Andrews sisters
sing from a convertible
my lover
shakes her pinup curls
no way José

shrimp and rice
are very nice
her voice goes sultry
to sing
c'est si bon

she kissed me
twice
morning glories
not even open
yet

snow melt
you find me
in the park
with a dog
I've just met

Venus
nearly touches
the crescent moon
come back, come back
my love

blond in a bikini
from the balcony
a sudden chill
beneath the clouds
goosebumps rising

on the treadmill
she sings a love song
to her iPod
the end
of my paperback

I zoom in
on the satellite
image
of your back yard
missing you

I scrub
a soup kettle
her new song
becoming
mine

her chilled fingers
seek warmth
under my sweater
one more house
to carol

martini olive
she sucks the liquor
out of it
and tries another
wink

green tomatoes
on the window sill
when will you
open up
to me

so easy to say
I love you
to a cat
with an empty
food dish

my heart
in the right place
she listens to it
over my
hairy warm breast

rocking on top
of the Ferris wheel
I ask her for
a wish as if
I could grant it

her whale
appears, disappears
now I know
it has everything
to do with me

old truck
with a loose clutch
good enough
for one more trip
to you

Army wife
tightens his scarf
as if he were
just going out
to walk the dog

the calm
of your voice
breaking up
in the confetti
of Times Square

an orchid
leans over the sink
three ice cubes
melting slowly
into her heart

not enough
for a country song
or a love poem
just her quiver
of moonlight

policeman's flashlight
reveals the startled faces
of moon lovers
one by one
cars leave the hilltop

barefoot under
the market umbrella
she picks up
a cucumber
to prove her point

magnolia buds
withered in their husks
I remove my gloves
to hold her hand
under a cold blue sky

new love ballad
I am getting to know
as you compose it
our old cat stretches
across a square of sun

she follows
my words
through the dark
winter night
to my good side

Dusty Old Bones

remember her
snowy day
visit to town
before we knew
the cancer?

transparent veins
of bean leaves
that's all
the beetles left
for me

the reach
of February light
who asked me to
carry these bones
so long

wild strawberries
on this Tennessee hill
how she lived
before her mother
died

a long winter
at her hospital bed
side
a hand in the hand
of the one

not feeding you
this time
young roosters
crowd
around my boots

we walk
around the farmyard
thinking of all
the things
to do, later

curled corn leaves
the old farmer
sifts dirt
from one hand
to the other

the death
nobody wants
to talk about
snow drifts
in the moonlight

I sit on the edge
of your old couch
afraid to sink in
like one of the family
nodding off to sleep

last car turns
into the cemetery
dust settles
over the blue
chicory

young lovers lying
in the sunshine
for a moment we
borrow their view
of the mountains

hot tub crowd
the old man
doesn't want
the young ones to see
his hobble out

blue dawn light
over new snow
you turn to me
for a word
of encouragement

half a stick
of gum
how you hurry
my answer
with a sigh

pulling out
what little hair
I have left
your king now
a wise old fool

faint rainbow
on a glacier
stone
we've run out
of words

a new face
at the corner cafe
not sure yet
who deserves
her smile

any day now
the gray sky will be blue
the saxophone
on the street corner
tells me it's true

looking for
the boy in me
I swing out
over creek water
on a groaning rope

you change stations
just as I
was getting nostalgic
a black thunderhead
looms ahead

shrimp
with garlic sauce
my name
at the campus
Chinese carry-out

a pair of ducks
splash in
I promise
to try harder
with new neighbors

a week later
grandma joins grandpa
we're all back
in the Kansas wind
on cemetery hill

old windmill spinning,
spinning with only
half the fins
coyote watches
from the scrub pines

on a whim
we turn
onto the dirt road
as if grandpa
was still there

all the flowers
gone stiff
seeds ready to fall
no matter how much we pray
she will be young forever

the turn
to grandpa's house
all the milkweed pods
merely shells
of themselves

mums deepen into
ruddy reds
and toasted yellows
singing acapella
she's so young at heart

the surgeon pokes flesh
and asks what hurts
here? how about here?
rain dripping
down the window

cigars on the deck
around the grill
fire and smoke
for such big boys
with big boy tales

up late
with a computer screen
rook takes pawn
my queen waiting
ever so patiently

farts
from town
to town
in a convertible
nobody cares

sparks
from the ceiling
little ones aim
their bumper cars
for grandpa

there they are
plain as day
locked up safe
my car keys
on the front seat

confident eyes
of dead flyboys
looking over
the relief map
of Iwo Jima

these hands
these steel-toed boots
what can I build
so the end is not
merely more dust?

you crack my skull open
and pick out
the bits of nut
walnut shell husks
at your feet

Vietnam veteran
so unusually silent
I check to see
if he's still
with us

old helicopter pilot
shuffles across the carpet
to his easy chair
a grimace with each
land fall

re-reading Psalm 23
it becomes her song
all night long
through the cold
through the darkness

in defense
of Rumpelstiltskin
she did get
three chances
and all that gold

a scar from Vietnam
no one else can see
the wings of a moth
fluttering
in a cobweb

home communion
I place the bread
on his tongue
ease the wine
over trembling lips

church elder
the sons and grandsons
look too old
to carry
his coffin

orange peel pieces
in the popcorn bowl
news from the war
so many names
we'll never know

flat headstones
of her parents
we brush dirt
and grass clippings
off their names

one of the young
in comparison
I spread out a beach towel
between a couple
of elephant seals

water flowers
pick tomatoes
deadhead
the marigolds
check check check

sanctuary . . .
ah, the piano tuner
knows
Moonlight Sonata
by heart

like riding a bike
she sets her arms
in a triangle
to stand on her head
for nephews

Captain Shirley
at the wheel
of our van
the granddaughters
aye-ayeing her

we follow
the hobbled over lady
sure enough
here it is
cool spring water

lights flashing
the sixteen wheeler
pulled over
for a dozen
ears of sweet corn

one by one
library lights off . . .
gently waking the lady
asleep with her face
in a dream

not a trace
of the farmyard
the garden
the hen house
just tumbleweeds

I try
to describe
her grandma's face
wilted peonies
on the grave

family photo
on the upright piano
her uncle remains
forever young
in uniform

Campus Rituals

students return
to campus
oh yes
now I recall everything
that's undone

wisteria
in the rain . . .
the professor lectures
on and on
about consolations

late summer
in the dean's office
I find a book of poetry
inviting me
to a floating world

midnight rain
on the kitchen window
another botched translation
of Basho's
lonely cricket

a survivor
of the great depression
she doesn't think much
of his poetry, but
he's handy around the farm

her sermon
of lilies in the valley
I start a haiku
then pray it into
a tanka

I show
the Zen master
my new poem
she shows me
her fist

after the Christmas
cookie party
the deans meet
for the New Year
budget cuts

spring break
I part my way through
arriving commuters
to the outbound trains
waiting on the tracks

the final draft
submitted to the professor
Socrates still
asking questions
in his head

dodge ball
in the park
graduates so eager
for another win
before moving on

Black Ant's Journey to Japan

spring rain
darkens
the airport runway
my narrow road
to Japan

one thing
at a time
a bite
of bamboo shoot
my whole tanka

shoes off . . .
stone steps
to the teahouse
cool
through my socks

thirty five
floors
over Tokyo
sun sets
in red wine

pulse
of white water below
sensei balances
on the exposed roots
of a tree

bus motor vibration . . .
tour guide's hand
blesses
each one
of us

wisteria
up the castle keep
I teach another
lullaby to
my housewife guide

begging bowl
empty
behind shrine glass
only dust in
his sake cup

suitcase
zips up . . .
crows talking
crow
in Tokyo

Walking the Fence

all the way home
through arctic wind
the moon
whispers
soon

not too late
for more water
for another pot of dirt
I want to give you
a thirst for sunshine

steeper and steeper
through slick wet
fallen leaves
are you sure
this is a trail?

to think
awhile longer
we sit on
this fallen log
world

seasons will come
and go
without me . . .
petals in
the paper weight

people say
I laugh all the time . . .
they're not with me
now that I'm
alone

lunch alone . . .
the fortune
cookie says
I'm sociable
and entertaining

blueberries
in the kitchen sink
she closes her eyes
to hear it
yes, the jenny wren

winter won't give up
I wait for warmth
to open my chest
into a prayer
for new life

black cat bone
and a mojo
tooth
who's gonna mess
with you?

full moon
the silent one
as we walk
and talk
along the river

a Luna moth
rises into summer night
everybody, all eyes
but mine
asleep

I hear
the rise and fall
of your dream
calm moonlight
across the yard

after the homily
the saxophone
takes us
on a closer walk
with thee

in line
at Taco Bell
suddenly God shows up
a little boy
comforting sisters

trillium
the tiny petals
catch snowflakes
for the father, the son,
and the holy one

somber morning
in the rain
enough time
not enough time
for twin towers

dust to dust
I take her hand in mine
and remember the smile
God loaned her
for a little while

into battle
with five smooth stones
and a sling
what more
could I pray for?

hibiscus bloom
will you be the one
to open up
to me
this morning?

death anniversary
she keeps her silence
all day
letting it go
in grace before dinner

a pear tree full
of white blossoms
in the bay window
a yoga master
cat

I climb Prophet's Rock
to look out
over the meadow
all the foxtails
a gathering of tribes

names of the dead
on the battle field
monument
not one of them
a Native American

green tongues
rise up
speak warm words
that cannot be said
by just friends

last catch
of the night
on the beach coals
where two or more
are gathered

rocks and sticks
for a little dam
again the mountain stream
finds another way
around me

a refreshing conversation
with a gorilla
at the zoo
I think we can be
best friends

Chinese painting
of a misty waterfall
in the corner
a poet the size of an ant
not going anywhere

my commentary
runs out at last
a flash of green
across the bay
at sun down

broken moon
I don't know
what to do
with all the pieces
of you

a song
about being born
to fly
if only her feet
could touch down

teen suicide
whispers through
the school
everyone knows
her name now

traffic jam
near the speedway
we follow Buddha
so calm, mounted
on a Harley

not a salute
just a nod
yes, I will
take care of
your little sister

Ash Wednesday
a prayer
for forgiveness
he is unable
to give himself

a long air walk
I never would have
reached you
without knowing
how to dream

folds of skin
open
a whale's eye
I have no names
for these constellations

About the Author

BRIEF BIOGRAPHY

Dr. Randy Brooks is the Dean of the College of Arts & Sciences and Professor of English at Millikin University in Decatur, Illinois. He teaches courses and workshops on haikai poetry traditions including haiku, renga, and tanka. His students' poetry and essays are available on the Millikin University Haiku web site: <http://www.brooksbookshaiku.com/MillikinHaiku/index.html>. Millikin University has hosted two haiku conferences: the Midwest Haiku Festival in 1992 and the Global Haiku Festival in 2000, which featured numerous guest haiku and tanka poets. The Tanka Society of America was founded on campus during the Global Haiku Festival. Dr. Brooks also teaches book publishing, serving as faculty advisor for the student-run book publishng company, Bronze Man Books, founded in 2006.

He and his wife, Shirley Brooks, are co-editors and publishers of Brooks Books and *Mayfly* haiku magazine. Randy and Shirley have been dedicated to publishing books, journals, bibliographies, and online collections of haiku in English since 1976 when they founded High/Coo Press. When they moved to Illinois in 1990, Randy & Shirley changed the name of the publishing company to Brooks Books. For more information about Brooks Books publishing see: <http://www.brooksbookshaiku.com>.

Dr. Brooks serves on the Executive Committee of the Haiku Society of America as the Electronic Media Officer. He serves as the webmaster for Modern Haiku Press and *Modern Haiku* magazine. He is on the editorial board for the annual Red Moon Press haiku anthologies. He also edits the web sampler issues and back issue archives of *Frogpond* magazine published by the Haiku Society of America. He serves as a member of the editorial team for the journal of haiku criticism, *Juxtapositions*.

Randy has won many awards for his poetry including 1st Place in the Harold G. Henderson Award from the Haiku Society of America. He and his wife, Shirley Brooks, co-edited *The Collected Haiku of Raymond Roseliep* which received the 1st Place Merit Book Award from the Haiku Society of America for books published in 2018. In addition to several chapbooks, a collection of his selected haiku, *School's Out*, was published by Press Here (Foster City, California). He and George Swede were co-editors of the *Global Haiku Anthology* published by Iron Press (England). Randy and Lee Gurga were co-editors of the *Midwest Haiku Anthology* published by Brooks Books. He and a team of students and former students were co-editors of the *Millikin University Haiku Anthology* published by Bronze Man Books.

Dr. Brooks been actively involved in building various archives of haiku publications and currently serves on the board for the American Haiku Archives in the California State Library in Sacramento. In the 1980s he edited and published four editions of *Haiku Review*, a bibliography of haiku books in print and current scholarship.

To facilitate research on contemporary haiku and tanka by his students at Millikin University, he established the Decatur Haiku Collection, with a complete bibliography of all holdings available on the Millikin University Haiku web site <http://www.brooksbookshaiku.com/MillikinHaiku/bibliographies/DecaturHaikuCollection.pdf>.

As Electronic Media Officer for the Haiku Society of America, he maintains the online collections of the Henderson Memorial Haiku awards, the Brady Memorial Senryu awards, the Einbond Renku awards, the Virgilio Memorial awards, the Museum of Haiku Literature awards, and the HSA Merit Book awards. He also manages the PDF library of back issues of *Frogpond*.

As web editor for Modern Haiku Press, he edited and designed a digital archive of the first ten years of *Modern Haiku* magazine, available on a CD. He has also completed digital archives of all issues of *High/Coo: A Quarterly of Short Poetry*, *American Haiku* magazine, and the growing web archive of *Modern Haiku* magazine.

Haiku & Tanka Collections by Randy Brooks

The Art of Reading & Writing Haiku: A Reader Response Approach. Brooks Books, (Taylorville, IL), 2019.

Broadside. *Haiku With Legs.* Brooks Books, (Taylorville, IL), 2015.

Common Time: Photo-Haiga. Limited edition of photography by Priscilla Meddaugh and haiku by Randy Brooks, Blue Connections Studio. (Decatur, IL), 2008.

Unmasking Us: Photo-Haiga. Limited collector's chapbook gift edition with photography by Priscilla Meddaugh and haiku by Randy Brooks, Blue Connections Studio. (Decatur, IL), 2007.

School's Out: Selected Haiku of Randy Brooks. Press Here, (Foster City, CA), 1999.

Broadside. *Crows Talking Crow,* [tanka] Press Here, (Foster City, CA), 1999.

The Homestead Cedars. The Virgil Hutton Haiku Memorial Chapbook Competition, (Normal, Illinois: Saki Press), 1999.

In Her Blue Eyes: Jessica Poems. (Decatur, Illinois: Brooks Books), 1998.

Online Book. *Black Ant's Journey to Japan: A Modern Tanka Journal.* (Gualala, CA: AHA Online Books), 1998.

The Collected Haiku of Randy Brooks. Boston Macintosh Users Group CD, Volume 2, Discovery Systems, (Dublin, Ohio), 1990.

Me Too! High/Coo Press, (Battle Ground, Indiana), 1985.

The Last Quarter Mile. Grey Whale Press, (Florence, Oregon), 1981.

Barbwire Holds Its Ground. High/Coo Press, (Battle Ground, Indiana), 1981.

The Rosebud Bursts. High/Coo Press, (Battle Ground, Indiana), 1979.

Where Will Mockingbird Nest? Juniper Press, (LaCrosse, Wisconsin), 1977.

HAIKU & TANKA EDITING & PUBLISHING BY RANDY BROOKS

Publisher, Brooks Books (formerly High/Coo Press), 1976-present.

Co-Editor with Shirley Brooks, *Mayfly*, 1985-present.

Web-Editor, *Modern Haiku: An Independent Journal of Haiku and Haiku Studies*, Modern Haiku Press, 2001-present.

Web-Editor, *Frogpond*, Haiku Society of America, 2008-present.

Editorial Team Member. *Juxtapositions: A Journal of Haiku Research and Scholarship*, The Haiku Foundation, (Winchester, VA), 2015-present.

Editorial Board, *Red Moon Haiku Anthology*, Red Moon Press, (Winchester, VA), 2005-present.

Editorial Board, Bronze Man Books, Millikin University, (Decatur,IL), 2006-present. Haiku and tanka titles include:

> *Winter Hearts* by Jackson Lewis, 2012.
>
> *Tea's Aftertaste* by Aubrie Cox, 2011.
>
> *Moon's Edge* by Natalie Perfetti, 2010.
>
> *Millikin University Haiku Anthology* edited by Randy Brooks, Emily Evans, Rick Bearce & Melanie McLay, 2008.

Editor. *The Hartsburg-Emden Haiku Anthology*, Hartsburg-Emden High School, (Hartsburg, IL), 2011.

Editor. *The Cardinal Haiku Anthology*, Warrensburg-Latham High School, (Warrensburg, IL), 2010.

Editor. *Modern Haiku*, Volumes 1-10 (1969-1979) on CD-ROM. Modern Haiku Press, (Lincoln, IL), 2010.

Editor and publisher. *Haiku: The Art of the Short Poem* by Tazuo Yamaguchi. A DVD/book by Brooks Books, (Decatur, IL), 2008.

Publisher, editor and book designer. *Lull Before Dark* by Caroline Gourlay, Brooks Books (Decatur, IL), 2005.

Publisher. *The Silence Between Us: Selected Haiku of Wally Swist*, Brooks Books (Decatur, IL), 2005.

Co-editor with Barbara Southard and Brock Peoples. *Dark Shade Flickering Sunlight: Selected Haiku of O Mabson Southard*, Brooks Books (Decatur, IL), 2004.

Editor and Publisher. *To Hear the Rain: Selected Haiku of Peggy Lyles*, Brooks Books (Decatur, IL), 2002.

Editor, *Harristown Haiku Anthology*, Flutterby Press (Decatur, IL), 2003.

Publisher and book designer. *Kiyoko's Sky* translated by Patricia Machmiller and Fay Aoyagi, Brooks Books (Decatur, IL), 2002.

Co-Editor with George Swede, *Global Haiku: 25 Poets Worldwide*, Iron Press, England, April 2000.

Editor and Publisher. *Almost Unseen: Selected Haiku of George Swede*, Brooks Books (Decatur, IL), 2000.

Editor and Webmaster, English-Language Haiku Web Site, Brooks Books (Decatur, IL), 1998-present.

Editor and Publisher. *Fresh Scent: Selected Haiku of Lee Gurga*, Brooks Books (Decatur, IL), 1998.

Foreword. "The Flow of Haiku." *Cur*rent: Linked Haiku by Marlene Mountain and Francine Porad* (Mercer Island, WA: Vandina Press), 1998.

Co-editor with Lee Gurga, *A Solitary Leaf: Haiku Society of America Member Anthology 1996*, the Haiku Society of America, 1997.

Editor. *Haiku: Season to Season*, Mt. Zion Intermediate School, Mt. Zion, IL, 1996.

Co-Editor with Lee Gurga, *Midwest Haiku Anthology*, High/Coo Press, Decatur, IL, 1992.

Editor, *MU Haiku, A freshman anthology*, Millikin University, 1990.

Editor, *Haiku Review, A bibliography of haiku publications and criticism*, High/Coo Press, (Battle Ground, IN), 1980-1988.

Editor, *High/Coo, A Quarterly of Short Poetry*, 1976-1982.

Publication Acknowledgments

Atlas Poetica: A Journal of Poetry of Place in Contemporary Tanka, 8, 10, 17, 21, 32, 34, (Perryville, MD), 2011–2018.

American Tanka, 23, 2013.

Brooks, Randy. *Black Ant's Journey to Japan: A Modern Tanka Journal.* Gualala, CA: AHA Online Books, (1998). Web. 1 April 2016.

Brooks, Randy. *Crows Talking Crow.* (Foster City, CA: Press Here), July 1999. [Broadside pamphlet.]

Bottle Rockets: A Collection of Short Verse, 9, (Wethersfield, CT) 2003.

Bottle Rockets: A Collection of Short Verse, 33, (Wethersfield, CT) 2015.

Bottle Rockets: A Collection of Short Verse, 34, (Wethersfield, CT) 2016.

Chhoki, Sonam, Editor. *Dream Alchemy.* Perryville, MD: Atlas Poetica, 2018.

Chhoki, Sonam, Editor. *Geography and the Imagination.* Perryville, MD: Atlas Poetica, 2014.

Cox, Aubrie, Editor. *Tea With Trolls.* (Muncie, IN), 2011.

Dirty Napkin 2.2, (Philadelphia, PA), 2009.

Dornaus, Margaret, and David Terelinck, Editors. *The Right Touch of Sun: Tanka Society of America Members' Anthology 2017.* Tanka Society of America, 2017.

Five Lines Down, 1.1 (Redwood City, CA), 1994.

Five Lines Down, 4, (Redwood City, CA), 1996.

Goldstein, Sanford, Editor. *Sixty Sunflowers: Tanka Society of America Members' Anthology for 2006-2007.* Baltimore, MD: Modern English Tanka Press, 2007.

Heron Quarterly, 2.3, (Escondido, California), 1998.

Heron Quarterly, 2.4, (Escondido, California), 1998.

Hummingbird, 5.4, (Richland Center, WI), 1995. Special issue featuring Sandy Goldstein.

Hummingbird, 6.1, (Richland Center, WI), 1995.

A Hundred Gourds, 4.3, (Web journal), 2015.

Kei, M. *Fire Pearls 2: Short Masterpieces of Love and Passion, Volume 2.* Perryville, MD: Keibooks, 2013.

Kei, M. *Take Five: Best Contemporary Tanka 2008.* Baltimore, MD: Modern English Tanka Press, 2009. Editorial team: M. Kei, Sanford Goldstein, Pamela A. Babusci, Patricia Prime, Bob Lucky, and Kala Ramesh.

Kelsey, Julie Bloss and Susan Burch, Editors. *Science Fiction Tanka and Kyoka.* Perryville, MD: Atlas Poetica, 2018.

LYNX, 25.3, (Gualala, CA: AHA Online Books), 2010.

Modern English Tanka, 2.1, (Baltimore, MD), 2007.

Modern English Tanka, 3.2, (Baltimore, MD), 2008.

Northwest Literary Forum, 24 (Portland, OR), 1997.

The Pebbled Shore: The Tanka Society of America Member's Anthology for 2009, (Baltimore, MD: Modern English Tanka Press), 2010.

Raw Nervz Haiku, 4.4, (Alymer, Quebec), 1998.

Red Lights, 4.1, (New York, NY), 2007.

Ribbons: Tanka Society of America Journal, 2.1, (Crescent, OR), 2006.

Ribbons: Tanka Society of America Journal, 5.3, (Crescent, OR), 2009.

Ribbons: Tanka Society of America Journal, 11.1, (Crescent, OR), 2015.

Rotella, Alexis & Denis M. Garrison, Editors. *Ash Moon Anthology: Poems on Aging in Modern English Tanka.* Modern English Tanka Press, (Baltimore, MD), 2008.

Siddiqui, Mohammed H., Editor. *Season's Greeting Broadside [Lake Theme],* (Baltimore, MD), 2007.

Simply Haiku, 4.2, 2006.

Skylark, 1.2, (North Yorkshire, UK), 2013.

Skylark, 3.1, (North Yorkshire, UK), 2015.

Cox, Aubrie, Editor. *Tea With Trolls.* (Muncie, IN), 2011.

Undertow Tanka Review, 12, (San Juan, Puerto Rico), 2017.

SEQUENCES PUBLICATION ACKNOWLEDGMENTS

Collaborative Tanka Trios & Quartets

"Cicada Chorus: A Tanka Trio" by Carmella Braniger, Randy Brooks, and Aubrie Cox, *Atlas Poetica: A Journal of Poetry of Place in Contemporary Tanka*, 10, (Chesapeake Bay, MD), October, 2011.

"Green Tongues: A Trio of Tanka" by Randy Brooks, Carmella Braniger, and Natalie Perfetti, *Dirty Napkin*, 2.2, (Philadelphia, PA), Summer 2009.

"Night Owl: A Trio of Summer Tanka" by Randy Brooks, Carmella Braniger, and Natalie Perfetti, *Modern English Tanka*, 3.2, (Baltimore, MD), Winter 2008.

"What Luck, A Summer Tanka Quartet" by Jackson Lewis, Carmella Braniger, Randy Brooks, and Joseph Bein, *Atlas Poetica: A Journal of Poetry of Place in Contemporary Tanka*, 8, (Chesapeake Bay, MD), May, 2011.

"What's Underground: A Tanka Quartet" by Aubrie Cox, Randy Brooks, Carmella Braniger, and Natalie Perfetti, *Skylark*, 1.2, (North Yorkshire, United Kingdom), Winter 2013.

"Where We Come From: A Tanka Quartet" by Jackson Lewis, Carmella Braniger, Randy Brooks and Joseph Bein, *LYNX*, 25.3, (Gualala, CA), October, 2010.

window open
to an autumn night
she asks me for
another
tanka